CHANGING MATTER
IN MY MAKERSPACE

by Rebecca Sjonger

CRABTREE
PUBLISHING COMPANY
WWW.CRABTREEBOOKS.COM

MATTER AND MATERIALS IN MY MAKERSPACE

Author:
Rebecca Sjonger

Series research and development:
Reagan Miller
Janine Deschenes

Editorial director:
Kathy Middleton

Editor:
Janine Deschenes

Proofreader:
Kelly Spence

Design and photo research:
Katherine Berti

Prepress:
Katherine Berti
Abigail Smith

Print and production coordinator:
Katherine Berti

Photographs:
iStockphoto: p. 10
All other images by Shutterstock

Library and Archives Canada Cataloguing in Publication

Sjonger, Rebecca, author
     Changing matter in my makerspace / Rebecca Sjonger.

(Matter and materials in my makerspace)
Includes index.
Issued in print and electronic formats.
ISBN 978-0-7787-4606-5 (hardcover).
ISBN 978-0-7787-4622-5 (softcover).
ISBN 978-1-4271-2046-5 (HTML)

     1. Matter--Properties--Juvenile literature. 2. Liquids--Juvenile
literature. 3. Solids--Juvenile literature. 4. Makerspaces--Juvenile
literature. I. Title.

QC173.16.S56 2018   j530.4   C2017-907630-2
                                              C2017-907631-0

Library of Congress Cataloging-in-Publication Data

Names: Sjonger, Rebecca, author.
Title: Changing matter in my makerspace / Rebecca Sjonger.
Description: New York, New York : Crabtree Publishing Company, [2018] I
  Series: Matter and materials in my makerspace I Includes index.
Identifiers: LCCN 2017057954 (print) I LCCN 2018004614 (ebook) I
  ISBN 9781427120465 (Electronic) I
  ISBN 9780778746065 (hardcover : alk. paper) I
  ISBN 9780778746225 (pbk. : alk. paper)
Subjects: LCSH: Matter--Properties--Juvenile literature. I
  Science--Experiments--Juvenile literature. I Makerspaces--Juvenile literature.
Classification: LCC QC173.36 (ebook) I LCC QC173.36 .S5645 2018 (print) I
  DDC 530.4--dc23
LC record available at https://lccn.loc.gov/2017057954

Crabtree Publishing Company

www.crabtreebooks.com   1-800-387-7650

Printed in the U.S.A./032018/BG20180202

Published in Canada
Crabtree Publishing
616 Welland Ave.
St. Catharines, Ontario
L2M 5V6

Published in the United States
Crabtree Publishing
PMB 59051
350 Fifth Avenue, 59th Floor
New York, New York 10118

Published in the United Kingdom
Crabtree Publishing
Maritime House
Basin Road North, Hove
BN41 1WR

Published in Australia
Crabtree Publishing
3 Charles Street
Coburg North
VIC 3058

CONTENTS

WHAT IS MATTER?

What do puddles, bikes, and rocks have in common? They are all made of matter. Matter takes up space and has mass. Almost anything you can imagine is matter!

STATES OF MATTER

People can find matter in nature, called natural matter. Or we can make matter ourselves. Matter has different forms, called **states**. This means that different types of matter are shaped or made up differently. This book looks at two of the main states of matter: **liquids** and **solids**.

Liquids

The water in this glass is a liquid. This state of matter can be poured. Liquids flow into the shape of their container, or the object that holds them, and fill its space. Water is natural matter. Humans do not make it. Other liquids are made by humans. Can you think of a liquid that humans make and drink?

4

Solids

Look back at the glass of water on page 4. The glass holding the water is a solid. Unlike liquids, solids cannot be poured. They keep their shape. Humans make drinking glasses. Can you think of a solid that is natural, or not made by humans?

Did you know that matter can change states? Humans make glasses by **melting** sand into a liquid, which is shaped into a glass, then cooled to become solid again.

Solids keep their shape. These solids do not take the shape of the basket that holds them.

These pencils are solids. What solids do you use to create things?

YOU CAN BE A MAKER!

Makers use all kinds of matter! They dream up new ways to use liquids and solids. They experiment with their materials. Keep reading to learn more about matter, and even discover how to change it.

TEAM UP

Makers work with others to come up with ideas. We can learn a lot from one another's ways of thinking. Makers also team up to share their skills and supplies. **Makerspaces** are the places where makers work together. Find out if your school or library has one. You could also set up your own space with friends!

No right or wrong!

There is no right or wrong way to be a maker. As you create, remember:

- There is no such thing as a silly idea. You never know what could lead to something great!
- Each team member is an important part of a project.
- Makers learn to solve problems when things do not go as planned!

Makers work together to solve problems and create new things.

MAKER TIPS

Are you ready to discover what you can make by changing matter? Be sure to brainstorm **at the start of each project. Take five minutes to come up with as many ideas as possible.**

MAKE A PLAN

Choose one idea to try first. Plan what you will do. But be open to changes and new directions! If you work with a team, listen to each person's ideas.

Project plan

1. Choose idea
2. Write down steps
3. Gather materials
4. Carry out steps
5. Reflect—did it work?
6. Write down ways to improve idea
7. Try again

Try writing down each step of your plan separately. This will help you stay on task as you work!

Help along the way

If you get stuck during a Maker Mission in this book:

- Think about what might happen if you used other materials. You could also try using the same materials in different ways!

- Take time to understand the goal of each mission. Try saying it in your own words.
- Break the mission up into smaller parts. Focus on solving one part at a time.

Remember, liquids fill the space of whatever holds them. They take on the shape of their containers. You could break or bend a solid to fit it into a container. It would not fill all the space, though. Solid matter keeps its shape instead of flowing.

DOES IT CHANGE SHAPE?

Snow globes show how liquids and solids are different. A solid container, shaped like a **dome**, holds the water. The liquid takes the shape of the container. Solid figures are also inside the container. They do not change shape.

DOES IT FLOW?

If you have a snow globe, give it a shake! Write down what happens. The liquid flows around the container. Solids, such as pretend snow, may move in the water. But they do not flow like a liquid. Other solids, such as **models** of people, plants, and animals, may stay in one place inside the container.

Try it!

Create your own snow globe to explore how liquids and solids move. Gather some friends to share ideas and supplies. Get started with the Maker Mission on the next page.

Some solid objects attach to the base inside a snow globe. This helps them stay in one place.

MAKE A SNOW GLOBE

Make a snow globe that holds a liquid and a solid. When your snow globe is complete, use it to explore these two states of matter.

MAKER MISSION

Materials

- Paper
- Pencil
- Clear container with a screw-on lid, such as a baby food jar
- One or more solids, such as a plastic toy, a model, clay shapes, or a toy car
- Glue, tape, or other binding material
- Water to fill container
- Small spoonful of glitter

GLUE

THINK ABOUT IT

Materials

Should you test whether your solids are **waterproof**? How could you do this before placing them in your snow globe?

Will the lid be the top or the base of your snow globe?

Design

Will your solids float in the water or be stuck in place?

Does it matter which order you add the solids and liquids?

Will you attach your solids to the inside of the lid or to the container?

What could happen if you do not screw the lid on tightly?

MISSION ACCOMPLISHED

Do you see how the states of matter in your snow globe act differently? Write down the things you notice. What could you try next?

When your snow globe works well, check out the Endless Ideas on page 30.

13

WHICH STATE IS IT?

It is not always easy to spot the state of matter. Sand can be poured, and it seems to take the shape of its container. But sand is not a liquid! It is made up of many tiny rocks. Each rock keeps its shape as it is poured.

HANDLE TO CHANGE

Some liquids act like solids. These liquids often flow very slowly. You can speed them up, though. The way they flow changes based on how we handle, or use, them.

These tiny solids act like liquids when they move together. They take the shape of the hourglass. Can you think of any other tiny solids that act like liquids?

GIVE IT A TAP

Has your ketchup ever been stuck in its bottle? It doesn't seem to flow like a liquid. But tapping on the bottle makes the ketchup act like a liquid—it begins to flow out. The blob of ketchup that comes out acts like a solid, too! It keeps its shape if it is left alone.

Try it!

Flip to the next page to make your own liquid that acts like a solid. Keep trying, even if things don't work out at first!

Ketchup is a liquid that can sometimes act like a solid.

MAKE A LIQUID ACT LIKE A SOLID

Experiment with a liquid that acts like a solid! Mix together cornstarch and water to see what happens. Then discover how to handle the liquid to make it hold its shape like a solid.

Materials
- 2 cups (480 ml) of cornstarch
- 1 cup (240 ml) of water
- Large bowl
- Mixing spoon
- Clear, sealable plastic bag

THINK ABOUT IT

Materials

What are some ways you could handle the liquid so it acts like a solid? Should you use your hands or another kind of tool?

Have you ever shaped play dough? Did you roll it, smack it, or flatten it? Try it with your mixture!

Size

Look at the amounts of cornstarch and water in the materials list. Why do you think it is important to measure how much you use?

Design

How would mixing cornstarch and water in a bag instead of a bowl change what you can do with it? Try it!

MISSION ACCOMPLISHED

Did you find out how to handle the liquid to make it act like a solid? If it is too runny, which solid could you add a little more of? There is more you can do with this odd liquid!

Go to page 30 for more ideas.

TEMPERATURE CHANGES

Matter can change states. What happens to a snowman when it gets warm outside? It changes into water! Snow is a solid that melts. It turns into a liquid when it gets hot enough.

CHILL OUT

You can also change matter by cooling its **temperature**. Many liquids have a freezing point. This is the temperature at which a liquid becomes so cold that it turns into a solid. A chocolate treat starts out as a liquid! It cools into a solid inside a **mold** that gives it shape.

ICE MAKER

Freezing liquid water forms solid ice. It can become anything from ice rinks to ice slides! Some makers use ice to create sculptures. These figures can be any size or shape. Each icy part is carved or made in a mold.

Try it!

Get out your mittens because the next Maker Mission is chilly. Be sure to kick off your project by brainstorming some ideas.

Find out more about how heat changes solids on page 22.

MAKE IT FREEZE

Make an ice sculpture! You must use at least three molds as you change water to ice. Arrange them to create something cool.

Materials

- Paper
- Pencil
- Water
- Molds, such as water balloons, rubber gloves, or plastic containers
- Freezer
- Metal spoon
- Camera

THINK ABOUT IT

Materials

What might happen if the water is not completely frozen?

How long do you think the ice shapes will last when you take them out of the freezer?

Size

How much room will you need to fit your molds in the freezer?

How will you get the ice out of the mold? What do you think would happen if you ran warm water over the outside of your frozen mold?

Design

What molds will you use to create ice shapes? Will you make your own molds or use ones that are already made?

MISSION ACCOMPLISHED

Did you create and arrange three or more frozen shapes? Take a photo before your ice sculpture melts!

Explore the Endless Ideas on page 30.

HEAT IT UP

Solids do not all change states the same way. Rocks stay solid at temperatures that melt ice. It takes a lot of heat to melt rocks! The temperature at which a solid melts depends on the materials it is made up of.

Beneath Earth's surface, there is extremely hot melted rock called magma. It sometimes comes above Earth's surface when volcanoes erupt!

NON-MELTING SOLIDS

Other solids do not melt at all. How does heated wood change? It burns! Other natural materials **rot** in the heat. Find out more about this process on page 26.

Try it!

Head to the next page for a challenge that changes the states of wax. Planning will help you to succeed at this Maker Mission.

MELT AND HARDEN

A solid that melts into a liquid can change back to a solid. Ask an adult to light a candle so you can see this in action. Candles are made of a material called wax. Notice how long it takes to melt the candle wax. How does the wax flow when it changes to a liquid? Blow out the candle. How long does it take for the wax to change back into a solid?

Notice the speed at which the liquid wax flows. How does this compare to the speed at which water flows?

MAKE IT MELT

Make a piece of art as you change the states of wax. Did you know that crayons are made of wax, too? Your project must use at least 10 crayons. You will change them to liquids and make art with the flowing wax! Then, make the wax solid again to save your creation!

Materials

- Paper
- Pencil
- Flat board or canvas
- Wax crayons
- Glue, tape
- Hair dryer
- Craft sticks

MAKE IT SAFE

Make sure an adult is with you when you try this mission. Never touch liquid wax! It is hot enough to burn your skin. Hold the hair dryer only by its handle.

THINK ABOUT IT

Design

How will you keep the crayons in place on your board or canvas? Remember, you cannot touch the hot liquid wax!

Do you want the wax to flow by itself? Or, will you use a tool of some sort to move it around?

Materials

How will you change the solid crayon wax to liquid?

Do you think the wax will harden, or become solid again, by itself? Should you cool it somehow?

MISSION ACCOMPLISHED

Did you melt, then harden the crayons? If not, did you try using a hair dryer to heat up the wax? Be patient! It can take a while for wax to melt.

Find more challenges on page 30.

CAN IT BE UNDONE?

Look back at the Maker Mission challenge on page 20. You could keep melting and freezing the same water. The changes that you make to the water's state can be undone. The same matter could make a lot of icy projects!

CHANGED FOREVER

Some changes to matter cannot be undone. Picture what happens when bread is toasted. It can't be un-toasted! The way it looks and feels changes forever. Other solids rot or break down over time. A squishy, black banana peel will never become firm and yellow again.

Take a walk outdoors to explore how matter changes in nature. Find plant matter, such as leaves and flowers. How do they change over time? Do they start to break down? Look at their shapes. Note if they curl up or change size. See if they stay the same color. How do they feel? Do they break easily?

Try it!

You can keep plant matter from breaking down. The first step is to bring it indoors. Then use your imagination! Get started on the next page.

MAKE IT LAST

When solids rot or break down, the change cannot be undone! Experiment with ways to stop plant matter from breaking down. It must keep its shape and not fall apart for two weeks or longer.

Materials

- Paper
- Pencil
- Plant matter, such as leaves or flowers
- Waxed paper
- Scissors
- Heavy object, such as a large book

THINK ABOUT IT

Materials

Should you work with plant matter that looks new or old?

Does it matter if the color changes? Will that affect its shape or strength?

Design

Which steps could you take to help it stay flat? Will this help keep its shape, too?

Where will you keep your plant matter? Do you think the temperature is important for this challenge?

MISSION ACCOMPLISHED

After two weeks, check your plant matter. Did you stop it from breaking down? Flip back to the Maker Tips on page 8 if you need help. When you meet your goal, try something new.

There are more ideas on the next page.

ENDLESS IDEAS

Take the next step in your Maker Missions with these ideas:

Make a liquid act like a solid

pages 16–17

- Use three times the amounts of cornstarch and water. Make sure you have a large container or bag to hold the mixture!
- What could you do with this much liquid that acts like a solid? Try walking on it!

Make a snow globe

pages 12–13

- Did you float or attach the solids inside your globe? Try doing it the other way.
- Can you think of any other tiny solids you could use for pretend snow? Try it! What happens?

Make it freeze

pages 20–21

- Which natural solids could you place in the water before you freeze it? What do you think will happen to them?
- Try measuring the water before you freeze it. Then measure it again after melting your sculpture. Did the amount of liquid change?

Make it melt

pages 24–25

- How many more crayons could you use to create a larger artwork? Could you change how you arrange them?
- What do you think would happen if you used another solid, such as a lollipop?

Make it last

pages 28–29

- Make a gift with your plant matter, such as a bookmark or a greeting card.
- What could you make by putting together multiple pieces of plant matter?

LEARNING MORE

BOOKS

Hurd, Will. *Changing States: Solids, Liquids, and Gases*. Heinemann, 2016.

Larson, Karen. *Changing Matter*. Teacher Created Materials, 2015.

Oxlade, Chris. *Changing Materials*. Crabtree Publishing Company, 2008.

· ·

WEBSITES

Find more fun ways to freeze water in maker projects:
www.cbc.ca/kidscbc2/the-feed/things-you-can-freeze

Follow these steps to create colorful art with melted wax:
www.52kitchenadventures.com/2011/09/12/melted-crayon-art-tutorial

Check out ideas for how to keep plant matter from breaking down:
www.kidsgardening.org/garden-activities-pressed-flowers-and-leaves

See how other makers create snow globes:
www.pbs.org/parents/crafts-for-kids/homemade-snow-globes

Learn more about the cornstarch and water mixture that acts like a solid:
www.scientificamerican.com/article/oobleck-bring-science-home

· ·

GLOSSARY

brainstorm To list many ideas—no matter how silly—as quickly as possible

dome A rounded structure shaped like half a ball

liquid Matter that can be poured and takes on the shape of its container

makerspace A place where makers work together and share their supplies and skills

mass The measurable amount of material in matter

material Any substance that makes up matter

matter Any material that takes up space and has mass

melt To change from solid to liquid

model A representation of a real object

mold A form used to shape a material

rot To break down or decay

solid Matter that does not flow and cannot be poured

state The form that matter takes, such as a solid or a liquid

temperature The measure of how hot or cold something is

waterproof Describes materials that do not take in water

INDEX

ABOUT THE AUTHOR

Rebecca Sjonger is the author of more than 50 children's books. She has written numerous titles for the *Be a Maker!* and the *Simple Machines in My Makerspace* series.